DEAR BODY

LOVE, ME

Jacquelyn B. Fletcher

GOLD HOUSE PRESS
Books and gifts to evolve the human spirit

Illustrations and text © 2016 Jacquelyn B. Fletcher
All rights reserved. Published 2016
Printed in the United States of America

Book and cover design by Cheryl Viker
Author photo by Joanna Proesser
Published by Gold House Press
P.O. Box 40, Lakeville, MN 55044
goldhousepress.com

To order in bulk or for wholesale pricing, contact the publisher at info@goldhousepress.com.

ISBN 978-1-941933-08-4

DEDICATION

To my gorgeous, sacred body.
Even after everything I've put you through,
you faithfully show up with your beautiful heart
and your lovely curves. Thank you.

Dear Body,

I am writing to apologize to you. I have hated you and starved you and pinched you. I have forced you to

eat too much and
then crucified
you for being
too fat. I have
examined every
inch of you for
your flaws. I
have used you
without regard

for your safety.
I have demanded
that you go
places you didn't
want to go. I
have given you
to jerks. I have
refused to
listen to you.

I have buffed and
polished you and
plucked and
shaved you. I
have made you go
without sleep,
without exercise,
without touch.
I have punished

you for your
love of wine and
dark chocolate.
I have allowed
other people's
words about you
to determine
how I treat you.
I have avoided
looking at you

in mirrors. I
have studied you
in mirrors with
the eyes of an
enemy looking for
weaknesses. I
have pushed you
to exercise until
you ripped.

I have stressed
you out so badly
you responded
with heart
palpitations and
insomnia. I have
ignored you and
turned away from
your pain.

I have done all
of this and more.

Dear Body,

Today I want to
say I'm sorry.
I'm sorry I've
made you suffer.
I'm sorry I've
made you feel
like you could
never be enough.

I want you to
know how grateful
I am that you've
healed yourself
again and again.
When I first
started listening
to you in a yoga
class I was
astonished.

You asked me to
be gentle with
you. You asked
me to be respectful.
You pointed out
all the beautiful
things about you
I had missed. You
reminded me that

you're fragile
and resilient. You
showed me how to
pay attention to
your needs and
to decipher your
messages. I learned
what certain aches
and pains were
warnings of.

I learned that
some foods made
you feel fantastic
and others didn't.
I learned to give
you enough sleep
and enough
exercise. You
showed me how
to lose

100 pounds and how to keep it off. I began to see how incredible you are, how miraculous with your trillions of cells made of stardust and spirit.

I saw you swell
with new life and
give birth to a
child of the
infinite awe.
I held her and saw
how extraordinary
her body was,
how beautiful,

how wondrous.
I saw her grow
and learn to
feed herself. I
watched her
discover her own
body's language.
She figured out
how to tell what

different tummy
aches meant ~ I'm
sick, I'm full,
I'm hungry, I'm
nervous. I knew
that I would
NEVER treat her
body the way
I've treated you.

And I realized
that I want to
change my
relationship with
you forever and
for good.

Dear Body,

You are astounding!

You are so strong

and so beautiful.

You are a perfect

example of how

cells and muscles

and bones and

blood can come

together to create a one~of~a~kind woman. You give me the ability to love, to hug, to hold on tight. You dance with discomfort. You warn me of

danger. You laugh.
You snuggle into
soft sheets and
pull a beloved
close. You breathe
in and savor. You
stretch and grow
and remember
the poses no

matter how long
it's been since
you've stepped
onto your yoga
mat. You ache.
You cry. You get
rejected and try
again. You show
up every time.

I call on you
to perform. You
tell me when I've
pushed you to
exhaustion. You
show me where
my fear lives.

Dear Beloved Body,

I honor you.
I vow to pay
attention to your
needs. I promise
I will listen as
you change and
age and sag and
lose steam.

I will not punish
you for being
who you are. I
will do my best
to love you in
the ways that
make you feel
loved. I will
ask other people

for help when
you need it. I
will bow with
deep respect to
your ability
to carry on. I'll
stop saying I'm
the kind of
person who

doesn't take naps.
When you're ill,
I will take time
off. When you're
tired, I will let
you relax. When
you're calling
to me, I won't

numb out. I
promise you I'll
let you experience
pleasure without
killing your joy
with shame.

Dear Body

Dearest Body,
Thank you!
Thank you for
your size and
shape. Thank you
for housing this
brain, this
heart, this spirit.
Thank you for

these hands,
these feet, this
stomach. Thank
you for these
magnificent
thighs and this
glorious ass.
From this day
forward, I will

tell you how much I respect you. I will share with you that I see how hard you work. I will honor your strength. I will give thanks for

Your mysteries.
I will nourish
you and take
you out for sushi.
I will make time
for laughter. I
will dress you
up in your
favorite outfit.

If the bra jabs
you in the armpit,
I won't wear it.
I will make you
feel like a
Goddess. I will
let you take
yourself less
damn seriously.

I will take things
off your shoulders.
I will ask for a
back rub. And a
foot rub. And a
full~body
massage. I will
put you to bed
early. I will

let you get up
without an alarm.
I will honor
your rhythms and
cycles and seasons.
I will make sure
you have enough
before I give
anything away.

I will raise your
gaze so you can
see. I will slow
down. I will let
you linger. I
will tell you
out loud and in
front of every~
one that

I LOVE YOU.

Dear Body,

Can you ever
forgive me?
Can you open your
heart to me
again? Will you
let me show you
how committed
I am to making

this relationship
work?

I LOVE YOU.

Dear Body,

I see now that

you are a miracle.

I hope you can

see I am a

changed woman.

I LOVE YOU.

Dear Body,

Will you give
me another chance?

Love,

Me

Acknowledgements

This book feels like life's work territory for me and it wouldn't have happened without Cheryl Viker who has said yes to so many ideas without batting an eye.

To Margie O'Loughlin and Brenda Berg. I am so thankful for the gift of your creative collaboration.

My husband, Arne, is my battery pack. My path is made so much easier with his presence and love.

My daughter, Evangeline, is my teacher and the greatest thing I've ever made.

My stepchildren, Connor, Cameron, and Chandler, have made my life exponentially richer.

Dr. Johanna Rian, Dr. Paul Scanlon, Rick Andresen and David Coleman at the Dolores Jean Lavins Center for Humanities in Medicine at Mayo Clinic have cheered for me and changed my life. They put a girl who was called "fatso" in front of a camera and helped her see her own talent and beauty.

Thanks to my friends who help me have the courage to talk about a topic that's close to the bone: Tara Jaye Frank, Tracy Sides, Maggie Knoke, Janet Sterk, Rebecca Longawa, Rick Monteith, Lara Cornell, Lindsay Walz, and the Gerasimo and Bacon clans. And to Stephanie Ross, Karen Olson, and Faye Castellano for helping me walk my spiritual path with greater maturity and grace.

To all of my yoga teachers. Each of you handed me a map. You taught me how to listen to my body and respect it. You showed me how to create a strong core and a strong heart at the same time. Namaste.

ABOUT THE AUTHOR

Jacquelyn B. Fletcher is an award-winning author and speaker. She's co-creator and host of the Healing Words television show and a founding faculty member of the Creative Writing at the Bedside program, both administered by the Mayo Clinic Dolores Jean Lavins Center for Humanities in Medicine in Rochester, Minnesota. She serves as Chair of the Board of Directors at the Loft Literary Center in Minneapolis.

Really, she's a transformation expert. She's lost 100 pounds and kept it off for nearly 20 years. Dug herself out of debt. And recovered from a broken heart again and again.

Her books and projects all aim to support healing, encourage empowerment, and inspire transformation.

Jacquelyn's powerful talks about body awareness and creative expression leave audiences inspired and armed with the tools they need to build confidence and create change.

To find out about having Jacquelyn speak to your group or to see more of her books and gifts, visit **JacquelynFletcher.com**.